The Ultimate *Twin Mom* 30-Day Devotional

Shawntae N. Nalley

TRILOGY CHRISTIAN PUBLISHERS
Tustin, CA

Trilogy Christian Publishers
A Wholly Owned Subsidiary of Trinity Broadcasting Network
2442 Michelle Drive
Tustin, CA 92780

The Ultimate Twin Mom 30-Day Devotional

Copyright © 2023 by Shawntae N. Nalley

Scripture quotations marked NLT are taken from the Holy Bible, New Living Translation, copyright © 1996, 2004, 2015 by Tyndale House Foundation. Used by permission of Tyndale House Publishers, Inc., Carol Stream, Illinois 60188. All rights reserved.

Scripture quotations marked CSB are taken from the Christian Standard Bible®, Copyright © 2017 by Holman Bible Publishers. Used by permission. Christian Standard Bible, and CSB®, are federally registered trademarks of Holman Bible Publishers.

For information, address Trilogy Christian Publishing

Rights Department, 2442 Michelle Drive, Tustin, CA 92780.

Trilogy Christian Publishing/ TBN and colophon are trademarks of Trinity Broadcasting Network.

For information about special discounts for bulk purchases, please contact Trilogy Christian Publishing.

Manufactured in the United States of America

Trilogy Disclaimer: The views and content expressed in this book are those of the author and may not necessarily reflect the views and doctrine of Trilogy Christian Publishing or the Trinity Broadcasting Network.

10 9 8 7 6 5 4 3 2 1

Library of Congress Cataloging-in-Publication Data is available.

ISBN: 979-8-89041-418-2

ISBN: 979-8-89041-419-9 (ebook)

Dedication

To my wonderful husband and high school sweetheart. Thank you for all the years you have dedicated to me and our marriage. You are an amazing man who has shown and taught me so much throughout our life together. Now you are an amazing father. Thank you for loving your daughters and I unconditionally. I could not begin to picture a life without you. Thank you for always being a wonderful leader of our home. You are an example of the Lord's precious love, and these girls have the very best Daddy! They absolutely love you and so do I! Thank you, baby!

To my sweet girls, Journey Nevaeh and Ryah Skye. Thank you for making me a mommy and filling my one heart's desire. I love you both beyond measure. May the Lord bless you in all you do. You were made for great things! I can't wait to see how amazing you are. May everything you set your heart out to accomplish, you do! I pray that you always know your worth! You are completely invaluable! Everything I do, I do for you. I hope you are proud of your mommy. I love you both so much!

Introduction

When I first became a twin mom, I went on a search for spiritual support. I knew that to travel this journey, I would need the Lord. There was nearly nothing to be found. The chances are you are a twin mom yourself who was also searching for something- anything. So, when I say nobody understands this journey like a fellow twin mom, you know exactly what I mean by that.

I had absolutely no idea what to expect when I saw two sacs on that monitor. The initial reaction was shock. We were literally speechless. I still have the video now. The doctor announced it was twins and you would have thought he was speaking to a non-hearing crowd of people. The silence was deafening. And then my husband breathed a sigh of what I believe was fear but maybe disbelief too. He said "yay" and the room broke into laughter. The doctor said, "Okay I was worried for a moment." It was a perfect memory to throw in the memory bank for sure. I can't wait to show my girls when they get old enough.

All I could think about is how much love and how many kisses we would share amongst the four of us. Oh, and all the cute matching outfits too. Except I was the mom that said I will NEVER match them identically, just coordinate them. Let me tell you, 99% of their life they match. It is like a rite of passage that twin/multiple moms have! So, we can own it. We knew right away, based on the ultrasound, they would be fraternal and not identical. Or so we thought. Did you know that even if they are dizygotic or "di/di" twins they could be identical? There was a thirty something percent chance they could have been identical anyway. Don't quote me on that percentage. It doesn't matter. My girls look nothing alike. So, we know they aren't identical. I had absolutely no idea how much of a whirlwind I would go through the next 365 days of my life. The ups and downs on a rollercoaster were no comparison for those twelve months. But equally the very best moments of my life that I will never forget. I will hold them in my heart forever.

I would be lying if I said there were not times in those twelve months, and even still, that I miss the pre-baby life. The times I had before the girls came along. The freedom. The privacy. The opportunities. Even the alone quiet time. And, my goodness, the sleep. But there is nothing I would change about my life now. I couldn't picture a day without these two nuggets. And I know you feel the same! I do wish they would go to sleep at a decent time, but apparently, I birthed night owls! They are like their momma! I feel the most productive when the sun goes down. I am not an early riser. Excuse me, I was not an early riser. But that is clearly no longer my choice.

This life is so much better now. Yes, so much has changed and so much has happened. But if I sit and think about my past long enough, I can see how I was empty and how these girls saved me. I can see how I allowed useless and meaningless things to fill up my time. Now, it is diapers, bottles, and baby sign language videos. Oh, and don't forget the sleepless nights, really early mornings, and sporadic sweet silent naps. Life is so beautiful and exhausting all at the same time. And you need to be okay with starting projects and having to pause them. You quickly learn how to jump back into those projects or restart them. This past year I haven't even really been able to cook dinner. If it is not one, it is the other, if it is not the other, it is both at the same time, screaming for my attention.

There is so much I know absolutely nothing about. So much to still learn. But one thing I do know is when I look into those beautiful eyes and see them smiling back at me, makes all the hard things worth it. It is a feeling that can't be replaced by anything else. That is the blessing of the Lord!

I hope you enjoy this 30-day devotional and find some quiet time to spend with the most important relationship of your life, the one with your Lord and Savior! I love you! I am for you! I pray the very best for each and every single one of you. I pray blessings over you and your precious littles! YOU GOT THIS! YOU CAN DO IT. YOU WERE MADE FOR HARD THINGS!

Contents

Note to the Reader xi

1: Joy 1

2: Fear 4

3: Anxiety 8

4: Happiness 12

5: Stress 16

6: Jealousy 20

7: Anger 24

8: Grace 28

9: Regret 32

10: Excitement 36

11: Patience 40

12: Worry 44

13: Identity 48

14: Love 52

15: Depression 56

16: Hope 60

17: Blessings 64

18: Loneliness 67

19: Bitterness 71

20: Faithfulness 74

21: Grief..78

22: Gratitude 82

23: Hopelessness 86

24: Kindness.................................. 90

25: Doubt.....................................93

26: Marriage..................................97

27: Comparison...............................101

28: Grace 105

29: Attitude 109

30: Healing 112

In Closing...................................121

A Note to the Reader

I love you, friend!

In this devotional you will find personal stories, discussion questions, and prayers to pray. I wanted to include some extra lines for you to answer the questions as well as a note section in the back. It is important for you to know that I have dreamt of this day of writing this for you. Well, at least for every day this past year. I don't know everything, but I do know the things I have been through. Things you may have also or will possibly go through yourself. Community is so important. I can't tell you how alone I felt during that first year. Even though I really wasn't. If it were not for the Lord, I don't know that I would have made it. There were so many moments that I was ready to just throw in the towel, but who knows what that really looks like. It is not like I could have un-birthed my children. They were here.

And life continued. But not without the Lord. Join me on this journey. I hope you find some encouragement in this. It is my heart to make sure you know how amazing you are. You can for sure survive the hard days and love and embrace all the wonderful days. The fact that you are reading this devotional tells me you are looking for support, so look no further. I am here. I pray the Holy Spirit lavishes His love on you each moment of this journey and you don't go a day without feeling it. I love you, friend!

DAY 1

Joy

I pray that God, the source of hope, will find you completely with joy and peace because you trust in Him. Then you will overflow with confident hope through the power of the Holy Spirit.
(Romans 15:13, NLT)

The moment I set my eyes on my baby girls my life changed forever. I knew there would be two, but I had no idea what exactly that would mean in real life. It was then that I heard the loudest cry ever. They brought that loud crying baby over to my face as my body lay there absolutely still. My arms were stretched out, IV's everywhere, and my abdomen completely open. I had to have a cesarean section due to positioning. I am sure that most other moms of multiples can relate to that decision already being made for them by their unborn children. I am assuming that is one of many. I wanted to have a natural birth. But they had other plans.

In that moment I experienced joy like I had never experienced it before. Then came the second cry. This time a totally different tone. A super sweet timid cry. Another healthy baby. The sweetest sounds a new mom could ever hear. You read about it. You hear about it. But until it happens to you, you have no idea! This my friend is real, true joy. And nothing could have prepared me for what was to follow, but for now, it was joy. The presence of the Lord filled that room. Everything else was silent but the sweet sounds of my new life. It was at this moment I felt the love of the Lord in a way I had never experienced it. It was perfection.

1. Describe the feeling you felt right after the birth of your babies whether at home or in the hospital.

THE ULTIMATE TWIN MOM
30-DAY DEVOTIONAL

2. What ways did the Lord show you joy during this
    time?

3. What was your best memory from that day?

Dear Heavenly Father-

Thank You for being true joy. Thank You for our babies. And thank You for showing me your presence when things feel difficult. I pray, God, that you would continue to bless me with the eyes to find and see your joy in all things. Becoming a mother was the hardest and best thing I have ever done. Thank You for healthy sweet babies. I pray that they always remain healthy and under Your wings! In Jesus's name I give thanks, Amen.

DAY 2

Fear

So do not fear, for I am with you. Do not be
discouraged, for I am your God. I will strengthen
you and help you. I will hold you up with my
vicious right hand.
(Isaiah 41:10, NLT)

I still remember the feeling I felt when we were officially discharged from the hospital. We were sitting in our room waiting for a nurse to come inspect the babies in the car seats. The same car seats that sat vacant for the last month in our car waiting for this very day. That is standard in most hospitals. They need to make sure they are in the seat appropriately. And let me tell you that is where the fear began. Did we put them in correctly? Will we pass this test? So many questions and no answers. I actually thought for a minute... what if they are not in right? Will they not let me take them home? I was exhausted.

This day was encompassed with fear. The fear of walking out of the hospital and putting these two tiny humans in our car and beginning our new life as parents. Two tiny babies that were solely dependent on us for not just diaper changes, cuddles, and bottles, but for survival. The fear of driving about forty-five minutes home safely was also a real concern. It seemed like there were extra cars on the road that day. The fear of not even knowing where to begin. And then there was the fear of getting home and starting this new life. We went from a family of two to a family of four instantly. Most people have time to warm up. They usually just add one. But not us! We go big.

The Lord and His faithfulness were all around us. I couldn't see it then and, in the moment, but He was. Looking back now I can clearly see that He surrounded us completely. We were not alone in this new endeavor. He has our entire future in the palm of His hands, and we were ready for it. Or so we thought. You are not alone on this journey. The God of peace is holding your hand.

1. When did you first feel fear after giving birth to your babies? Or did you even feel fear?

2. What ways did the Lord show you joy during this time?

3. What was your biggest fear after arriving home with your babies?

Dear Heavenly Father-

Sometimes, the spirit of fear comes in to overtake us. Help us to remember to call on You in those moments. We don't have to be alone; You are with us, and You are for us. So, who can stand against us and prosper? We aren't promised an easy life, but we are promised that You are going to be with us every moment of the way. In Jesus's name I give thanks, Amen.

DAY 3

Anxiety

Don't worry about anything; instead, pray about everything. Tell God what you need and thank him for all he has done.
(Philippians 4:6, NLT)

I distinctly remember pulling into our driveway with these two new babies in tow. Knowing very much that once we enter the house our life will never be the same. It kind of felt like we walked into a room that was a huge mess and we didn't even know where to start. You spend months preparing for their arrival just to find out you are not at all prepared. I remember praying, "God these are your children, help me to be a good mom to them." I also remember the amount of anxiety that flooded my body as well. I knew what I pictured life to be like, but I did not know my picture was a fantasy. Sometimes, anxiety, when left alone or ignored, can be completely debilitating. And if left alone too long can also grow into something that is overtaking. You don't want your anxiety to turn into depression. Because trust me it can.

That first night was the hardest night of my life. I don't think we slept at all. The girls were up probably every two hours. I can still remember begging God for at least a three-hour stretch. We were exhausted. We were overwhelmed. And we were filled with anxiety. Let's just say that three-hour stretch would be a long time coming. I can remember getting up multiple times throughout that night to confirm they were breathing. In those early days I experienced twenty emotions all at the same time. Many people warned me of SIDS. I don't even want to go into what that is. If you are unaware, you can Google it. Praise God for His faithfulness and love. The road to motherhood is most certainly the most anxiety ridden one you will ever take. But GOD.

There were moments where I thought that God left me. Things felt helpless and I couldn't see how any of this would work. Maybe I was not supposed to be a mom. Maybe I was really in over my head. But the Lord showed up in every way possible. He loved on us in ways that I can't even explain. He will be there for you. He will not leave you. So cast that anxiety on Him and He will undoubtedly carry you through. God has a plan for you and your babies that you may not see yet, but I can promise it is a beautiful one. You are worth all the amazing things.

1. Recall the moment you pulled into your driveway. How did you feel? What was going through your mind?

2. What ways did the Lord show you joy during this time?

3. Did you rely on yourself to pull out of that place of anxiety? Or did you rely on the Lord?

Dear Heavenly Father-

Thank You for always being our constant. Our point of contact for unconditional love. Thank You for always being there no matter how far we drift. Lord, we know You are the one who can conquer it all. Help us to remember to cast our cares and anxiety on You. And not on ourselves. Your words are clear in Proverbs 3:5-6, Lean not on your own understanding but in all Your ways acknowledge Him and He will lead you on your path. It is why You sent Jesus, to die, so we didn't have to carry it. Thank You, Jesus. Amen.

DAY 4

Happiness

Make me walk along the path of your commands,
for that is where my happiness is found.
(Psalms 119:35, NLT)

While the first few weeks after getting home were the hardest of my entire existence on this planet, it was also the happiest. I, for the first time, experienced real true happiness. I could stare into these little girls' eyes for hours. I could just sit and watch them sleep. I could find comfort in the rise and fall of their chest. Breathing meant I was doing something right. We tried for fourteen years to get pregnant with no success. Every cliché piece of advice you can think of we heard and more than once I can assure you. "Just relax." "Don't try." "Just adopt, plenty of kids need a home." Blah, blah, blah. All good intentions, I am sure just more hurtful than they knew. Oh, and don't forget Mother's Day. For fourteen years I hated that holiday. It was so awkward. Especially when people would wish me a Happy Mother's Day. I made it a point to always lay low. Now it is my favorite day of the year. I know I have earned it! Anyway, I am getting ahead of myself.

After much prayer and waiting we decided to take the next step into IVF. May of 2021, we dove right in and became pregnant in September 2021. The first round, the first try. It worked. The process was a difficult one. The medications. The shots. The pain. The unknowns. It was all so hard but then when we found out that it worked on our first try, it was complete happiness. That was 100% God. And then God needed to show off. He decided we could handle twins. Doubled the blessing we waited for. We clung to the scripture in Joel that says, He will repay us for all the time the locusts took. We were living the absolute dream. Two babies. It was like God gave us both a baby to have for ourselves. We were drowning in happiness.

We were surrounded by love. Even in the hard moments. Even when we were so tired, we couldn't remember if we had even had dinner or not, we were engulfed in love. It is easy and natural to love your offspring. It is certainly instinctual. I knew when I looked at them in the face that they were my body, my flesh, my very own creatures! We made these. And they were inside of me. God will show you happiness at every turn if you look for it. It is up to you to use those eyes of love and seek happiness. If you look for a red car on the street, chances are you will see so many red cars. That is the same for happiness. If you seek to see that, the positive parts, you will find them. God is in every single moment of that. I picture Him smiling at us and even saying to himself, "I told you I would do it." And He did. He did it.

1. What was the most exciting part after bringing your babies home? Where did you find the most happiness?

2. What ways did the Lord show you joy during this time?

3. Describe the reaction you and your husband had when you discovered they would be twins!

Dear Heavenly Father-

You are the prince of peace. You are where happiness comes from. It would be unhelpful for us to try to find happiness in people. You gave us these precious babies to be stewards and caretakers of and that has brought us happiness. Help us to see the joy in their eyes when they gaze into ours. Even on the hard days and sleepless nights You are still good and there is still so much happiness. In Jesus's name I give thanks, Amen.

DAY 5

Stress

From the ends of the earth, I cry to you for help
when my heart is overwhelmed.
(Psalms 61:2, NLT)

I once read that the Chinese use "sleep deprivation" as a form of torturing and punishment while doing interrogations. If you have never had a baby, you may not understand this. But allow me to be the first to tell you directly, it is terrible and real. After the birth of the girls, sleep deprivation was the biggest hurdle. Oh, and then there is one of our girls being lactose sensitive and colicky. This is especially hard with twins. Why? There is no break! Two babies. Two parents. No break. Either one baby wakes up the other or by the time you get the one down, the other then wakes up ready for a feeding.

There is a terrible feeling when laying down, covering up and getting perfectly comfortable just so the other wakes up and you start the process again. Diaper, feed, burp, rock, and hopefully sleep. This process took a lot longer than we would have liked. It's not like with one baby where you could take turns with dad. Switching nights back and forth. That sounds like a walk in the park. But not us. Not the twin parents. When I say this causes stress, I mean this can bring a relationship to its knees quickly.

Another huge stressor is a crying baby. A crying baby that you cannot get to quit the crying. A crying baby that you can't determine why is crying. Not only will the noise itself make your bones tingle but all the things that go with it. The fact that the crying baby will inevitably wake the sleeping baby. The fact that you have no idea why, so you have to go through a checklist and exhaust every idea. It is hard! I started to tell myself that she was crying because it was her way of singing. She is going to be a future singer. And that is what I am sticking to.

God is the master of time and after this journey, I will never question His timing again. I don't think my marriage would have survived fourteen years ago if we had a baby when we first started to try. So, trust His timing and believe He does know best. And He does love us so much. And this sleep deprivation will end. I spent so much time praying while dealing with all those wake ups. I still do now. God has always been in the midst of this all. He has never left me or forsaken me. And He won't leave you either! He always shows up for us and He is always on time when He does!

1. What was the longest you went without sleep? What did you do to get through this time? How did you survive?

2. What ways did the Lord show you joy during this time?

3. How did you feel when you started to get longer stretches of sleep?

Dear Heavenly Father-

The reality is life can't exist without some kind of stress. There is so much that causes stress. The best part is that You are already in those situations before we are. Thank You for being on my side as we navigate this new life full of new stresses. Help us from allowing unnecessary stresses. We can't control everything so we will only focus on the things we can control. It is not easy but with You holding my hand and guiding my steps, I know we can conquer it all. In Jesus's name I give thanks, Amen.

DAY 6

Jealousy

A peaceful heart leads to health in the body, jealousy is like cancer in the bones.
(Proverbs 14:30, NLT)

I dreaded this topic the most. It makes me feel unhappy with myself on so many levels and even more so, guilty for feeling this way. While I am not making excuses, I am being honest when I say that we are humans, and we all have and experience emotions we are not particularly proud of. We all say things we wish we could take back. We all feel ways we wish we didn't. So, for that I say... thank God for His grace and love. I thank Him for His forgiveness! I have never really had any previous issues with jealousy in my life. Not until my babies were born. Apparently, they were not the only thing I gave birth to. Apparently, I also gave birth to this new and slightly foreign emotion.

Life isn't always so simple. Allow me to explain how this correlates with this topic. A couple of my friends had babies shortly after I had the girls. They had one baby though. I must admit they have had it pretty easy. And seeing that while we were sinking was difficult. Our entire life had been flipped upside down and nothing really changed for them. They still did all the things they did before their babies were born. They weren't sleep deprived. They weren't stressed. They didn't appear to be suffering at all. They were able to take breaks. Empty hands for just a moment. The complete opposite from our current situation.

Let me tell you the enemy is the author of comparison. It causes unnecessary stress and robs you of your joy. If you allow it. I found myself so jealous at times I even felt for a brief and embarrassing moment, cursed. It is hard for me to even admit that out loud. I thought my two blessings were a curse. I can't believe I thought that. I do regret that I allowed this thought to take root in my mind. I still have my moments where I am like, *I wonder what it would be like if I only had one?* But the reality of this statement means one of them would not be here if that were the case and I can't imagine my life without either one of them. At times, I feel ashamed for feeling this, but I also realize that it was the enemy hard at work trying to steal the joy the Lord gave us.

We waited fourteen years to feel this joy and the Lord overflowed our cup. And I have the audacity to complain? No. That isn't going to work. So just know if you have had or are currently having these feelings, they aren't yours. It is not how you really feel. It is just the tactic of the enemy. He is trying to steal your joy.

The Lord picked you and I to have this double portion of blessings because He loves us. And He deemed us worthy for this journey.

1. Have you ever had a time where you experienced feelings of jealousy?

2. What ways did the Lord show you joy during this time?

3. Write a moment when you felt this way and then when you gave it to the Lord.

Dear Heavenly Father-

We all experience our moments of weakness. Help me to turn to You in those moments. Block out the spirit of jealousy from my life. It has no place. Rather fill it with love. You are the one that blessed us. Forgive me for spitting on this blessing. You gave me two of the most beautiful gifts I could have imagined. And for them, I thank You so very much. Help me focus on being a better mom and the situation I do have rather than the situation I don't have. I love those babies beyond measure. In Jesus's name I give thanks, Amen.

DAY 7

Anger

*And "don't sin by letting anger control you." Don't
let the sun go down while you are still angry, for
anger gives a foothold to the devil.*
(Ephesians 4:26-27, NLT)

During those first few days after getting home, I was
trying to recover from my c-section. I was in pain and
very exhausted. I am so blessed that I have an amazing
husband and life partner who took the reins and did everything I couldn't do. Walking was hard. Sitting up was
hard. Going to the bathroom was hard. And all of that
made me so angry. Seeing my husband do everything, I
could see all the exhaustion on his face. He was doing all
the things I wanted to do. I felt so helpless. I gave myself
no grace. The fact was I just had a very major surgery
and I still couldn't see that. I was angry that my body
was keeping me from being a mom. I was ready for it to
be healed and get back to normal. But my body just was
not ready yet. I went through so many emotions dur-

ing that time. I was sleeping on a couch next to the crib where my new babies were sleeping.

It was this time that the Lord met me in such a beautiful way, He used my husband to speak words of love and encouragement straight into my heart. He lovingly and with tears in his eyes explained that the enemy is attempting to steal our joy and we must not let him. I need to focus on healing and building a bond with my new little girls. And I vowed to do just that. I couldn't rush my healing no matter how much I wanted to. So, I had to do what I could while taking care of myself. I kept my eyes on the Lord and my heart on my babies.

Prayer was the most important out for me. As well as journaling. I have to write everything down. Keeping the Lord in my forefront. It was hard going through these emotions at times. I didn't really understand them always. I felt happy because we were finally getting what we wanted. Yet, I can't do anything to do the things I want to do to help out. I had to put my focus on the Lord. I had to trust in His timing and His process. I knew I needed to heal. So, I just had to go with the flow. I knew that the Lord was in control, and He had me in His hands. He is so good!

1. Was there ever a time that you felt so angry that you lost your joy?

2. What ways did the Lord show you joy during this time?

3. What did you do to get rid of that anger? Did you turn to the Lord, or did you rely on yourself?

THE ULTIMATE TWIN MOM
30-DAY DEVOTIONAL

Dear Heavenly Father-

We face situations daily that cause us to be angry, but only if we allow them. We are in control of what makes us mad and what we dismiss. Help us to not accept those feelings of anger. Let our lives be so filled with love that there is no room for much else let alone anger. Thank You for showing us that love conquers all, especially anger. Just like Your word says, don't let the sun go down while we are angry. In Jesus's name I give thanks, Amen.

DAY 8

Grace

Each time He said, "My grace is all you need. My power works best in weakness." So now I am glad to boast about my weaknesses, so that the power of Christ can work through me.
(2 Corinthians 12:9, NLT)

During that first month our church community and friends showed us the love of God and His precious grace in so many ways. They showered us with cards and meals. I can't thank them enough for how very helpful that was for us. How would we have time to prepare meals let alone eat them?

We could barely go to the restroom. This was one of the most amazing signs of God's presence in our new life. We were never good at accepting help. We had offers to help clean, help do our laundry, and to pick up groceries. Even though, we never really accepted any of those offers, which I regret now. It was a wonderful feeling to know that they were there for us. The Lord was using them to help us. They were acting as the hands and feet of the Lord. We still aren't very good at asking or accepting help from others, but we are learning. We also don't want to block anyone else's blessings. If people want to be a blessing, who are we to stop them? We don't want others to stop us from blessing them.

Another form of grace is something I needed to demonstrate towards my spouse. There is so much stress and interruption during this time in our lives, it was easy to get annoyed or upset with each other. Our life had literally been flipped upside down and now we had to learn how to operate as a family of four rather than be concerned with just the two of us. It was an adjustment. So, we needed to extend grace to each other. Add a little bit of sleep deprivation and boom we were in for a rocky road. Thankfully we made it through the first year. It wasn't easy but it is worth it. I am so thankful for God's grace towards us. We needed it that is for sure. He will keep you as well. Just use those times you feel crazy to spend time in prayer. It does help. And you are worth it. Give yourself grace, sweet friend, and to those around you.

1. Describe the feeling you felt right after the birth of your babies whether at home or in the hospital.

2. What ways did the Lord show you joy during this time?

3. What was your best memory from that day?

Dear Heavenly Father-

Thank You for being true joy. Thank You for our babies. And thank You for showing me Your presence when things feel difficult. I pray God that You would continue to bless me with the eyes to find and see Your joy in all things. Becoming a mother was the hardest and best thing I have ever done. Thank You for healthy sweet babies. In Jesus's name I give thanks, Amen.

DAY 9

Regret

But just to forgive us our sins and
to cleanse us from all wickedness.
(1 John 1:9, NLT)

I would not be completely honest with you if I said
that I didn't have moments of regret. And this is actually really hard for me to admit. When things started to
get challenging my thoughts began changing, and not
for the better. I allowed bad thoughts to creep in and
unpack for a bit. Questions filtrated my mind. "What
in the world did we do?" was one of the biggest ones.
Prior to this we had a pretty great life. We could sleep
and even sleep in if we wanted. We could actually watch
television or play on our phones. We could do our hob-
bies. My husband is an amazing guitarist. He often
would play at our church. I absolutely love puzzles, reading, writing, painting, and Bible journaling. I created
a Facebook group called Bible Doodling for Beginners
Ministry and Fellowship. I spent so much time in that

group creating and learning and just loving on the Lord and His people. It goes without saying I have not done many, if any, of these things since the babies were born. We can no longer come and go as we please. The fact of the matter is our life is no longer our own. And let me be clear that is a hard pill to swallow. Our life would never be the way it once was. And that is also another hard pill to swallow. But the reality is that it is now better.

The thought that I regretted having babies was a strong one at times. However, the Lord taught me that these feelings were not my own. They were just an attack from the enemy trying to steal my joy and happiness. The Lord was repaying us for what the locusts had eaten, and I was giving it all back by allowing the enemy a foothold in my life. The enemy was trying to get me to believe that this is how I really felt. But in reality, it was the opposite. I couldn't picture my life without our precious babies. I love them more than I love myself. And that is what is real. The Lord will always reveal the truth to you. He will not let you believe false narratives. This is His plan for you, and He wants and will make sure you enjoy it to the fullest.

1. Have you ever had feelings of regret? About what? How did you overcome them?

2. What ways did the Lord show you joy during this time?

3. Have you had to deal with the enemy putting bad thoughts in your mind? What was your defense against that?

Dear Heavenly Father-

You know my heart. Help me to discern what is real from You and what is a lie from the enemy. I do not have to give way to him and his attacks on my mind. Help Your word stand out to me above all things. Thank You for loving me even when I don't deserve it. Even when I start to momentarily believe the bad thoughts. And thank You so much for helping me see the truth. YOU are the truth and the life! In Jesus's name I give thanks, Amen.

DAY 10

Excitement

Give thanks to the Lord, for He is good!
His love endures forever!
(Psalms 107:1, NLT)

As our beautiful girls began to grow, there was so much excitement. Every checkup we went to the girls were knocking out their milestones early. Each report was literally perfection! We have been so blessed. Their head growth, their eye movement, length, and weight. Each appointment brought so much excitement. We were actually doing it. We were doing things we had no idea we were capable of. From the moment you hold your babies in your arms, you do anything you can possibly do to be the best parent you can be. It was exciting when they started rolling on time, crawling on time, and then walking on time. All before one. So, celebrate all of your progress. In fact, celebrate every day you survive because let's be honest as a twin mom, it is about survival! I mean it. Celebrate all the big and small successes.

I never want to forget these little things. When they first said, "da da," we were so excited. When they started to develop their personalities. Almost right away you could tell who would be the dramatic one and who would be more laid back. Holding their own bottles, putting their pacifiers back in their own mouths, feeding themselves their snacks were all exciting times as well. We want them to develop independence just as much as we want them to always need us in some way. Most importantly, we want them to know and love Jesus. So, take my word mama, get excited. Love on those babies. Enjoy the good moments. Share Jesus and His love for you and for them as much as you can. Teach them to be excited about life and all it has to offer. A relationship with Jesus will be the best relationship outside of the one with you that they will ever experience. Not to mention it will mold them into loving, caring, and respectful individuals. Raise them up to be followers of the King.

SHAWNTAE NALLEY

1. What are some of your most exciting memories from the first year? Which is your most favorite?

2. What ways did the Lord show you joy during this time?

3. How have your successes encouraged you so far on this journey to motherhood?

Dear Heavenly Father-

There have been so many hard moments throughout this past year, but You have been in every single one of them, never leaving us alone. Among those hard times we have had so much to be excited about. So much to be thankful for. We are raising the next generation of young people. Help us to be excited about and find joy in our day-to-day living as well as our children's future. We don't have to have specific moments to be excited. We have the best blessing in the world, children. Thank You for trusting us to be the parents of these precious babies. In Jesus's name I give thanks, Amen.

DAY 11

Patience

*Rejoice in our confident hope. Be patient in trouble
and keep on praying.*
(Romans 12:12, NLT)

This is probably one of the harder things for us to discuss. I am guilty as a new mom of losing my patience. My first year has been filled with many apologies, from me to my girls. I want to teach them that when they are wrong, they need to apologize. We all know the crying can get overwhelming. The constant wake ups. The endless diapers. Then that eventually turns into the "no-no" and the "stop that." Oh, and don't forget the "don't pull her hair," and "stop the biting." It is honestly all a perfect recipe for losing your mind and your patience. I have had some less than desirable and even a bit embarrassing responses myself. In fact, I won't even go into details. But as I mentioned earlier, I have repented and apologized profusely. The biggest thing that has come out of all this is that I recognize that I do need the Lord and without Him I am lost. I need the Lord to help me with self-control and help to respond appropriately and not the way my flesh wants me to.

I do need to make a statement here though, I have never hit or hurt my girls. I also want to state that I don't necessarily believe in spanking. I don't even really understand it. We can't hit people who don't listen to us in real life scenarios. So why would I do that to my children or teach them to do that? I don't believe that inflicting pain in an effort to get someone to do something I want them to do, or not do something I don't want them to do makes sense. This is where I needed and still need to rely on the Lord the most. I need Him in every moment of every day.

You are doing an amazing job and the Lord sees you and He loves you so much! We know that each season has its easy moments and then it has its less than easy moments. But what we also need to know is that God chose us for this time and these babies. No one can do a better job being the parent to, (insert children's names), than we can. God picked us! He chose us!

1. Has there been a time where you instantly regretted something you said or did when losing your patience?

2. What ways did the Lord show you joy during this time?

3. What did you do, or do you do, to prevent yourself from making the same mistakes?

Dear Heavenly Father-

I am so far from perfect. I am actually just the opposite. But You, You love me, and You never leave my side. I am so thankful for Your grace and Your forgiveness. I repent from all the times I have lost my cool and have became overly upset. I want to be a good example to my girls on how they should respond to anger and adversity in their lives. Patience is so important in all areas of our life. Help me to lead my girls with grace and love. Help me be slow to anger. I want to live according to Your will for me. In Jesus's name, I give thanks, Amen.

DAY 12

Worry

*But when I am afraid, I will put my trust in you.
I praise God for what He has promised. I trust in
God, so why should I be afraid? What can mere
mortals do to me?*
(Psalms 56:3-4, NLT)

I remember very vividly when my girls got sick for the very first time. They were four months old and so tiny. I was an absolute wreck. I can still hear the sounds of their coughing and wheezing. The congestion was so bad they couldn't even sleep, not to mention didn't know how to clear their throats. I have never worried about anything so much in my life. They took turns for the worst. My sweet girl, Journey, needed to be held all night long. It feels like yesterday. I held that baby all night long on my chest and I didn't sleep a wink. Feeling her breathing was my purpose. They never had fevers, but they were so helpless and pitiful. Runny noses. Crying and coughing and clinginess. It was just all so much. As a new mom that was my biggest fear and then when it was a reality, I was beside myself. All the mom groups on Facebook made me aware of RSV and that scared me to my core.

There is nothing worse than a sick baby, oh wait there is, two sick babies that are unable to take medicine or to tell you how they are feeling and what is hurting. Worry was my home for these few weeks. Sure, I prayed. Sure, I begged God for a speedy recovery. But I also worried too. It was one of those *give it to the Lord and then pick it back up again*. I think we can all admit to doing this at some point. We want to micromanage God. We say we love Him, and we trust Him but, then we question Him. We are constantly trying to take control and to take things into our own hands and do them with our own power.

Needless to say, I have had to learn to surrender my worry and my babies to the Lord. I know He is in control, and He can handle our biggest worries. I took my girls to the doctor just as any new and paranoid momma would do. I found out what everyone was already telling me, they were getting better and on the mend. The reality is this was the first of many years of worry to come. But what makes the burden of worry a little lighter is knowing God is in control of our little ones. In fact, He actually loves them more than we do, if you can believe that. So, give that worry to the one who has your babies best interest in mind.

1. Can you remember the first time you felt really worried about your babies?

2. What ways did the Lord show you joy during this time?

3. How did you feel after you realized that you were carrying the weight of worry and surrendered it?

THE ULTIMATE TWIN MOM
30-DAY DEVOTIONAL

Dear Heavenly Father-

Thank You for always showing up in my time of need. It is a refreshing feeling to know that I am not now, nor will I ever be alone. You are in full control of our hardest situations, and You want the best for our children. You love them more than we ever will and that is so hard to put into perspective. Help me to always surrender all of my worry to You and not pick it back up. Fill me with trust in You and Your plan for my family. We were not made to carry the weight of worry, that is precisely why You sent Your son to die on the cross. I love You Jesus, and Your love for me and my family. In Jesus's name I give thanks, Amen.

DAY 13

Identity

*My old self has been crucified with Christ. It is no
longer I who live, but Christ lives in me. So I live
in this earthly body by trusting in the Son of God,
who loved me and gave himself to me.*
(Galatians 2:20, NLT)

After becoming a mom so much of my life has
changed, actually, if I am being perfectly honest, every aspect of my life has changed. You know what I am
saying. For a few months I didn't even look like myself. I had absolutely no time to myself or for myself.
My permanent hairstyle was a messy bun. And not the
cute kind. I brushed my teeth. Daily. But that was the
only thing that was a guarantee in my life. The thought
of even shaving my legs was a foreign idea. I probably
could have braided my leg hair it was so long. I know
that sounds bad, but my life was not my own any longer.
I wasn't Shawntae as I knew myself, I was now Journey
and Ryah's mom. I can tell you that I have forgotten to

eat at times. I have waited to go to the restroom until it began to hurt. Life became and has been totally about them.

Bottles and diapers and schedules filled with pediatrician appointments were my life now. How many wet diapers? How many poopy diapers? How many bottles and how many ounces? Don't forget to make sure the diaper bag is packed and has everything that we could possibly need. Needless to say, if you are reading this devotional then you understand where I am coming from. You have been there, are there or you will be there at some point. I say all that to say that I completely lost who I was. My identity was "mom" and not Shawntae. Still at a year old there are many things that I have not been able to do that I love. I haven't been able to work on my Bible doodling, leisure reading, puzzles, or painting. I still have not made time for these. If you could see how I have managed to write this devotional, you would giggle. The majority has been in a parking lot, drinking a latte, or during nap time.

The truth is that I never lost my identity. The Lord just blessed me with an additional title. I gained more experience in life and added to my identity. The Lord so graciously showed me that I am exactly who He has made me to be. And He felt me worthy of not one, but two precious babies. And He feels that way about you too! We just need to get that in our heads! Don't let the enemy trick you into thinking that you are no longer yourself. You are just a new and improved self. A little busier self. A little less time for yourself self. And that is all temporary. I had my girls at thirty-six years old. For those thirty-six years, I have been my own. But now I am in a new chapter of my life. And it is the one that the Lord has for me just as are you.

1. Did you feel like you lost yourself after your babies were born?

2. What ways did the Lord show you joy during this time?

3. What ways have you been able to get your life back to "normal" or ways you have been feeling back like yourself?

Dear Heavenly Father-

Thank You for showing me who I am and whose I am. I am Yours! And my real, true identity is in You and does not change due to life's circumstances. I am thankful for that You are the God of my life and I love You so much. I can put my faith and trust in knowing that You, Lord, are in control and have me right where You want me. In Jesus's name I give thanks, Amen.

DAY 14

Love

*For this is how God loved the world: He gave His
one and only Son, so that everyone who believes in
Him will not perish but have eternal life.*
(John 3:16, NLT)

As it would turn out, love really does conquer all
things. God's love is so beautiful and encompassing.
And it is exactly what I needed to feel during these earlier months after bringing home the girls. As a new
mom you dish out so much love. Essentially you give
all of yourself and become slightly empty. I know you
hear that "self-care;" is important and I don't disagree,
but let's be honest, who has time for themselves while
juggling the care of two very new and needy babies?
You don't feel like yourself physically nor do you feel
like yourself emotionally. You are on this chaotic rollercoaster. You are up with all the love and support and
cuddles and then you are down with the blow-outs, colic, and sleepless nights. Nothing about this process is

easy, except for the love you feel for your babies. That is the easy part. No matter how tired you feel, no matter how much crying there is or how many poopy diapers, the love comes naturally. You never really know how much you can love someone or something until you give birth to a child. The unbelievable love I had for my dog paled in comparison to the love I feel for my babies. When they hurt, you hurt. When they are happy, you are happy. You just marvel in the love of these two precious souls.

After the smoke settles and the visitors die down and all the food gets eaten up, it will just be you and your babies. The two bundles of joy. Your very own miracles. The lives you created and carried inside of you for whatever that duration was. And they will stare into your eyes as if they have never seen anything more beautiful and you will do the same. Because the truth is you haven't seen anything like this ever before. This is what dreams are made of. You will sit there and dream of the things to come. You may even have moments where you will wish some of the hard moments away but trust me the time goes so fast. You will blink and it will be gone, and they will be big, and it will be all new challenges. But the love only grows and gets stronger. And God's love will radiate throughout your home. And it will all only get better and better as you go on. Each season has its own kind of hard, but it won't be anything you are not equipped to deal with. That is a gift from the Lord. He will carry you through all the hard times and bless you with so many good times. Enjoy the moments. Enjoy the love. You deserve it.

1. When was it that you felt the most love during this journey so far? Was it in the hospital? Was it when you arrived home? Or maybe even weeks later?

2. What ways did the Lord show you joy during this time?

THE ULTIMATE TWIN MOM
30-DAY DEVOTIONAL

3. Have you felt the Lord's love during the hard times? What did you do when you were not feeling love?

Dear Heavenly Father-

Your Word says that You are love. And that is the most valuable love we will ever need. Thank You for instilling a sacred love for our children inside of us. Help us to fix our eyes on that. On the sweet precious unconditional love that You have for us, and we have for our children. Help us love them the way You love us. God You are so faithful in all You say and do. Give us peace to know that You are in control, and You have us in the palm of Your hands. Nothing will ever change that. We can have confidence that You have our children in the palm of Your hands as well. In Jesus's name I give thanks, Amen.

DAY 15

Depression

This is my command- be strong and courageous!
Do not be afraid or discouraged. For the Lord your
God is with you wherever you go.
(Joshua 1:9, NLT)

Becoming a new mom and leaving your old life behind can be a sobering feeling. It is genuinely hard. So hard it can cause you to even fall into a depression. I did. I struggled so much. Any time I would close my eyes, I would be imagining how my life once was and pretending it is not what it is now. We can easily get wrapped up in the "what ifs" and the "if onlys," causing us to miss what is right in front of us. The here and now. Our new beautiful life. The life we prayed for. The life we waited so long to finally experience is finally here. Of course, we had no idea how hard it would be. If we had known what this would look like, then we would not have prayed for it.

After the first couple of months, I started to really go through it. I was sleep deprived. I was pumping or nursing every two to three hours. I had absolutely no time for myself. I dressed like I was homeless because I lived in spit up, drool, and even some explosive poops. I had no time for my life. For my own breathing. I felt like I was a robot going through the motions. I was feeding, pumping, changing diapers, changing outfits, rocking, burping, and getting only thirty-to-forty-minute increments of sleep. Even if you know that it won't last forever, in the moment it feels like it will. And that can be so depressing. It all feels so heavy. And even a bit like you are drowning. It is a lonely place.

The important thing is to know and understand that you don't really feel this way. The enemy is trying to steal your joy. The reality is it is hard, but it won't always be hard. You must lean on the Lord to get through to the next season. Each season has its joys and its challenges. You just have to embrace it all. The good. The bad. And everything in between. Just remember God is good and He is faithful. And most importantly He is not leaving you, ever. Take delight and knowing you will never be alone. It also helps to have people that you trust and that you can talk to. The truth is moms of singletons will never really truly understand. But that is no reason why you should not confide in a friend or family member to speak to. I was really blessed to have great friends at church as well as my sister-in-love. She was there for me to talk to when I felt super alone. I am very thankful; I love her so much. Just remember the Lord knows what you need and who you need when you need them.

It is also important to know that there is a stigma when it comes to getting help, taking medicine, or talking to people. Don't let anyone make you feel that way. I will be the first to admit. I finally agreed to take a low dose antidepressant. I am not saying I am an advocate. I am saying you need to do what you need to do to be the best you can be for your children. So don't worry yourself about what others think or believe. You need to pray about it and let the Lord lead you not others' opinions. You are worthy and deserve to feel good. God is so faithful when it comes to resetting your mind if you will surrender to Him.

1. Was there a time when you felt depressed or anxiety after having your babies?

THE ULTIMATE TWIN MOM 30-DAY DEVOTIONAL

2. What ways did the Lord show you joy during this time?

3. What methods did use to cope with your depression?

Dear Heavenly Father-

I don't have to tell You just how bad I feel some days. You are there before I am. You are always next to me and never leave my side. So, I am never alone as I go through these harder moments. Some of these emotions are due to chemical imbalances, but You are the Master Physician. Lord correct anything in me that is off with my hormones and restore me to Your perfect creation. Thank You for loving me, especially when I have a hard time loving myself. I love You, Lord. In Jesus's name I give thanks, Amen.

DAY 16

Hope

*Now may the God of hope fill you with all joy and
peace as you believe that you may overflow with
hope by the power of the holy spirit.*
(Romans 15:13, NLT)

It is easy to get mixed up and lost in your emotions. There is one thing that we need to be reminded of, we serve the Prince of Peace. He is the hope we have. We can look to Him to be filled with all joy and peace. My husband and I had many nights where we would get three to four hour stretches of sleep, and as minute as that sounds it would bring us hope. Our baby A, Journey, was colicky and we really struggled with her. She would cry for hours on end, and we had absolutely no idea what to do for her. We tried so many different remedies. It seemed like nothing worked. Eventually, but not quickly, we figured out that it was her formula. I then felt horrible because I realized that this sweet baby of mine was suffering. She was in pain all that time and

I was unaware. Finally, we found a formula that worked and that gave us hope.

Do you see the pattern? Hope doesn't have to be one big thing. It can be many small things. The point is the Lord loves us so much He gives us these blessings to keep our hope. If we are intentional when looking, we will find hope all around us. I can recall feeling so lost when she would cry and cry. I felt like it would never end. I felt like a terrible mom who couldn't even console her own baby. But once the new formula kicked in, things changed so much. They became a different kind of hard. A new season. But one that was so much more tolerable. I had hope for a better future.

Someone once told me "A storm won't last forever," and as simple as that sounds it was so profound. It really resonated with me. It was a true statement. Eventually the storm stops. Now I just see my trials for what they are and rejoice in them. James 1:2 says, "Consider it a great joy, my brothers and sisters, whenever you experience various trials, because you know the testing of faith produces endurance." I love that. What a verse filled with hope. There is hope my friends. Keep your faith and know it is all going to work out for your good.

1. What were some of the harder things you faced
    that attacked your hope?

2. What ways did the Lord show you joy during this
    time?

3. In what ways were you reminded of the love of God
    and the hope he provides when you faced those
    harder times?

Dear Heavenly Father-

We have absolutely nothing if we don't have hope. But because of You, the Prince of Peace, we have hope. A hope that is unlike any we could get from anyone or anything else. Thank You for being who we can turn to when we begin to feel hopeless. You have our entire future in Your hands. We have so many reasons to have hope. And You are the one that gives it and You give it unconditionally. I love You, Jesus. Thank You so much. In Jesus's name I give thanks, Amen.

DAY 17

Blessings

I will make you into a great nation.
I will bless you and make you famous,
and you will be a blessing to others.
(Genesis 12:2, NLT)

From the moment we took our two babies out in public, we knew we had something special. Everywhere we go we are told how blessed we are. Still to this day without exaggeration, at the age of one, we still have people constantly commenting about them. There has not been one day as of yet where we have not had a comment of some sort regarding our babies. I am not even inflating this. 99% of the time it is positive and uplifting compliments, but we have our fair share of stereotypes and negativity. "Double trouble" and "You got your hands full," are by far the most popular amongst the crowd. How original right?

I firmly believe that these encounters are God's little reminders for us to see that these girls are a blessing.

THE ULTIMATE TWIN MOM
30-DAY DEVOTIONAL

Even in the hard times. They are blessings. It makes the hard moments a bit more tolerable. Don't get me wrong, there are times where I lose my cool. I recognize the error of my ways, repent, and work towards change. Another reminder is the fact that I know people who are praying for what I have right now. Even twins.

I remember in those fourteen years of trying and praying and waiting, I would have love to be able to complain about a hard day. So, I know where I came from. I am humble enough to admit that I know where I came from. The point is that if we shift our thoughts, we will shift our life. If we focus on what God wants for us, we will change our whole outlook. The truth is your babies are blessings and made for this time. And you were picked to be the mom of these perfectly imperfect babies. There is no one else who could be a better mom to those babies than you, my friend. Have confidence in knowing the hard moments will pass and you will lavish in the love of Jesus.

1. Write out a situation where you realized that you are really blessed by having two babies.

SHAWNTAE NALLEY

2. What ways did the Lord show you joy during this time?

3. Have you ever experienced comments out in public that you had to bite your tongue on?

Dear Heavenly Father-

Your word says in Psalms 127:3 that children are a gift and a reward. Thank You so much for seeing me worthy of a double portion. Lord, You love me enough to allow me to raise and nurture these sweet babies. I won't take this position for granted. Help me to remember during the hard moments that these babies are a blessing. Help me to be a good mother and raise them right to know You and to love You. We will always choose You first in our home. In Jesus's name I give thanks, Amen.

DAY 18

Loneliness

The Lord is close to all who call on him,
yes, to all who call on him in truth.
(Psalms145:18, NLT)

Every moment with these babies is a blessing. I am blessed to be alive and blessed to be the one they will call mom. I could not imagine spending a day in my life without them now that they are here. I most definitely could not picture myself dropping them off anywhere. Not at a school nor a day care not even a relative. The decision to be a stay-at-home mom was a joint one between my husband and I. At first, before their arrival, I was unsure. It sounded ideal. But then once they were here there was absolutely no way I could do it.

Being a stay-at-home mom is certainly a lot harder than it sounds. I know most people, especially ones without kids, think that being a stay-at-home mom is just coffee, lounging, and binge-watching Netflix after a nice afternoon nap. Let me tell you how complete opposite that is for me and probably most other moms of multiples.

It can also be a very lonely job. Sure, you are with your babies all day, but they don't speak adult. By the time my husband gets home I am so exhausted I don't even want to talk. I don't want to stay up any length of time after they go to bed. I am too tired to even think about being intimate. I am just exhausted, and it is a lonely place. You will begin to feel like a failure as a wife.

The constant crying, the being needed, the diapers and the bottles. Spit up and poop explosions. All the while not really having anyone to talk to. So, I encourage you to stay connected and reach out to friends. Try to stay in your church small groups. Even if all you can do is zoom calls, I say do it! The lonely feeling will go away. You will feel better. It only stays hard if you let it. Don't become a recluse. I am the CEO of isolation; you will only do yourself harm. Know, until you get in a routine, the Lord is certainly near you. You will never be alone. That is a promise I can make to you. So don't think that for a second. And know there are many of us out there feeling the same.

THE ULTIMATE TWIN MOM
30-DAY DEVOTIONAL

1. Have you ever felt like you were lonely on this journey? What did you do to help get out of that funk?

2. What ways did the Lord show you joy during this time?

3. Are you a stay-at-home mom? If so, do you regret this decision? If you aren't, do you wish you were?

Dear Heavenly Father-

There have been many times I have felt alone. And all the while You have always been right there by my side. Your word says You will never leave me, and I believe that. You have proven Your faithfulness time and time again. I love You, Lord. You are my best friend and because of You I never have to be alone. In Jesus's name I give thanks, Amen.

DAY 19

Bitterness

Let all bitterness, anger, and wrath,
shouting and slander be removed from you,
along with all malice.
(Ephesians 4:31, CSB)

I remember the exact way I felt when my husband's paternity leave was up. He was home for six weeks which was a huge blessing in and of itself. That first day was absolutely terrifying. Two babies. One me. All alone. Depending on me, needing me, crying, screaming, and pooping. I was on pins and needles, and I could feel the anxiety building up in me as he got ready for work. He grabbed his protein shake, kissed me and the girls, and was out the door. But there I was. All alone. Day in and day out. I would be up all night with him taking care of babies. Then I would be with them all day by myself.

However, my husband got to go to work. He could get out. Escape the noise. For a brief time early on I was drowning in bitterness towards him. Yes, he was going to work so he wasn't getting a "break" in the sense of being able to rest, but he was getting a "break" from the crying and constant caring for a baby. Put one down and get another one. I was jealous of him. Why did he get the freedom? Why did he get to breathe?

Then came my heart to heart with the Lord where He lovingly reminded me that my girls are a blessing. I don't have to be their mom. I get to be their mom. And I don't stay home with them because I have to, I get to stay home with them because I can. My husband is the sole provider of our home, and he needs to work. After my mindset was reset, I began to behave differently as well as feel different. I have felt blessed ever since and no longer bitter towards my husband. Sure, I have moments of weakness where I fantasize about getting out and working a job outside of our home, but then I see those perfect innocent faces staring at me as if they have seen the most beautiful thing in the world. And there is no better feeling.

1. Have you ever felt bitter or negative towards your spouse? If so, why?

THE ULTIMATE TWIN MOM
30-DAY DEVOTIONAL

2. What ways did the Lord show you joy during this time?

3. What was your biggest take away from feeling this? Do you still struggle with this? What do you do about it?

Dear Heavenly Father-

Lord, help us to know that sometimes we have feelings that are not the truth. You are the truth. Show us the best way to look past these feelings and temporary emotions. Allow us to be happy for our spouse that they are able to get a break. Our time will come, and we will enjoy all the moments up until then. Remind us how much we truly love and care for our spouses. Fill us with Your kind of unconditional love. Thank You so much, Lord. In Jesus's name I give thanks, Amen.

DAY 20

Faithfulness

Because of the Lord's faithful love we do not perish,
for His mercies never end.
(Lamentations 3:22, CSB)

There are many days where I would wake up already exhausted. It seemed like day in and day out I was a robot on autopilot. I still feel like that sometimes. The thought of all the things the day held was utterly exhausting. And the reality is you are never really ready. But you know it must be done. After all, you have two humans that depend on you, maybe more if you are not a first-time mom. You are their lifeline. They can't do anything without you. They need you for love, nourishment, and care. You can't take the day off. There are no sick days in the mom industry. And most of the stuff you need to do and get done can't be put off until tomorrow. Maybe a load of laundry or a vacuum but that is pretty much it. You have to get up. Show up. And do the things.

What I can say is when it really mattered God's faithfulness was always there. How? People. He uses people. In the low moments when I was at a loss, God would send someone to show up for me. They would show up to help. They would show up to bring a meal. They would show up to hold a baby. I am very blessed to have such an amazing mother-in-love who literally moved in with us during the weekdays. She set her life aside and showed up for us. Spending the night, waking up with babies, feeding, changing, and helping cook. She was the perfect example of God's faithfulness when we needed Him the most. Her help was invaluable and irreplaceable. Aside from my husband, no one could have loved those babies like we did but her. My sister-in-love even spent a few months pregnant at first then with her newborn, coming over to help. She had a singleton so it was a little more manageable for her to do things I couldn't do. But she loved them perfectly.

The moral here is God sees you just the way he seen me. He shows up. I can give you my word, if you look, He will be there. And He will use people to love on you. You just have to be open to that.

1. What ways did you see God's faithfulness when you needed it? Did you not see it then and see it clearer now looking back?

2. What ways did the Lord show you joy during this time?

3. Did you ever feel abandoned by God in the earlier days? How did you feel when you realized He was there the entire time?

Dear Heavenly Father-

You are faithful, there is absolutely no question about that. Give us the eyes to see You when our human eyes can't. We have experienced You, Your love, and Your faithfulness firsthand. No one could change our minds about that. Thank You for being the one constant thing I can rely on no matter what. In Jesus's name I give thanks, Amen.

DAY 21

Grief

The Lord is near to the brokenhearted;
He saves those crushed in spirit.
(Psalms 34:18, CSB)

Having twins brings out a grief inside of you, you never knew existed. Maybe after any child but I can only speak on twins, as they are my first. There is a somber feeling knowing you will never be the same. That sounds so dramatic, but it is so real. Your life will never look like it was before you brought a life or lives into it. Your new normal is that you are no longer the priority. At least not for a long time. I used to get my nails done every two to three weeks. I used to keep up with my roots every three months. I was able to get up and exercise, grab a coffee, and come home to relax. Read a good book. Put together a puzzle. Watch sermons. Bible journal. Facetime my best friends. I was a director of a team of one hundred in a multi-level marketing business that I loved. It has been over a year now and I have done maybe two of those things I just listed.

With all that said, not to worry, this is just a season. I remember thinking that I needed to grow up now. Because of our infertility we had kids later in life. And while those last fourteen years felt like torture, it was for our own good. I don't think my marriage was ready right away. We needed that time to build a solid fire-proof marriage. And for the last thirty-six years I got to live the way I wanted. So, it is not like I missed out. I could do anything and everything I wanted. Now I get to be a mommy to two amazing, beautiful girls who I get to do new fun things with.

Sure, we miss sleeping in. Dropping everything to just go out to dinner or hang out with friends. Spend time talking to adults and watching adult movies like Courageous, Fireproof, and Facing the Giants. Now it is early mornings, planning meals, and baby sign language. Those things I used to be may just be distant memories but now we get to make new ones. And they are totally worth it. Memories like those first baby giggles, cuddles, and then the first "mama" and "dada," it makes all the hard moments worth it. We made it a year. And you will too. Don't allow the memories of the past to keep you from living in and enjoying the right now. Your babies will never be this age or size again. Once this time is gone it is gone and I imagine that will be a whole new level of grief. Cast your cares on the Lord. He has you covered. He loves you so much and will make sure you remember all of these perfect moments.

1. Do you ever find yourself feeling grieved from moving into this new life?

2. What ways did the Lord show you joy during this time?

THE ULTIMATE TWIN MOM 30-DAY DEVOTIONAL

3. What about your prebaby life do you miss the most? What about your current life do you love the most?

Dear Heavenly Father-

Lord, thank You for this new busy chaotic life that You trust me with. Help me to never forget You chose me to be the mom of these perfect souls. We are deeply blessed. Yes, our life may look different now but a better different. Help us to keep our eyes focused on You and the blessing of it all. Not the life we no longer have. The new beautiful life we are blessed to live. In Jesus's name I give thanks, Amen.

DAY 22

Gratitude

*And let the peace of Christ, to which you were also
called in one body, rule your hearts.
And be thankful.*
(Colossians 3:15, CSB)

The news of a formula shortage began to spread quickly. I couldn't believe it. After all these years of not having kids and we finally do and now there is a nationwide formula shortage. And after we finally find the right one for our sweet baby girl, Journey. I really wanted to nurse my baby until a year and then I found out that I was having two. It seemed like an impossible task. Not to mention my girl, Journey, didn't want me. Aside from the rejection I felt from my baby, I felt like a terrible mom. But she had so many digestive issues that she needed that hypoallergenic formula. I was only able to nurse my "baby b," Ryah. And that only lasted eight and a half months. I was really proud of myself because it was such a challenge. I did the best I could.

Sometimes, I think I could have tried harder, but I did my best for the moment I was in.

I ended up joining a group on Facebook that I am extremely grateful for. It was a formula search group. A group of moms would go to different stores and take photos of the formula aisles and share them. If you see one that had your formula, they will often purchase it for you and get it to you. We were blessed enough to find someone a few cities away whose Walmart continuously restocked our formula for a bit and so we would drive an hour to go get it. Then when that ran out, we actually met someone who used the same and her family would travel from New York to bring it back for her. So, she brought us some as well.

The gratitude I felt for the Lord for using a complete stranger is beyond words. You never know how He will come through for you, but you can be confident that He will. He is always on time. Needless to say, with the woman by the Walmart and the woman with the family member, we had enough to get us by. Finally, we were able to get her on a regular formula that was always fully stocked. That was a huge relief. And also, I believe another blessing from the Lord. He knew what we needed and when we needed it and even used complete strangers to provide for us. God will provide for you. Trust Him. He is worthy.

1. What is something that you have been very grateful for?

2. What ways did the Lord show you joy during this time?

3. Has there been a time you started to feel nervous about something and then God showed up for you?

THE ULTIMATE TWIN MOM
30-DAY DEVOTIONAL

Dear Heavenly Father-

You never let us go without. Thank You for all that You do and continue to do for us. Especially when we least expect it. You are always on time. Help me to not get worried in the waiting. What a blessing it is to be a daughter of the one true king. I love You, Lord. Help me to always see Your blessings right in front of me. In Jesus's name I give thanks, Amen.

DAY 23

Hopelessness

He brought me up from a desolate pit,
out of the muddy clay, and set my feet on a rock,
making my steps secure.
(Psalms 40:2, CSB)

As I mentioned in the previous devotion, we went through a really hard time with our baby, Journey. She got colic right about six weeks old, and it lasted for about three months. That three months felt like it was an eternity. She really struggled. The endless hours of crying are hopeless ones. The inability to make your child happy is a hopeless feeling. The inability to take away their discomfort and pain is a hopeless one. And the inability to explain what is happening is a hopeless one. Those months dragged on forever. Those moments can have you questioning everything.

I spent many nights crying myself to sleep and feeling like I ruined my life. And if I am transparent with you, I still have my moments of weakness where I feel like I had it all together and then I had babies. This is not the life I envisioned. I wanted three or four kids but after having two at the very same time, I don't know if I want to be done. After you get out of those really hard times you often wonder if you want to take the chance and start again. That is certainly a gamble. I will tell you we were really blessed to have our second baby, "baby b," be a super easy and content baby. This would make anyone question; if we did it again, which one would we end up with?

If you aren't careful, you can get trapped into wishing away the time. You begin to feel like the hard moments mean a hard day or week or even month. But the reality is they are just that. Moments in time. A blink of an eye. It is easy to feel hopelessness when you are right in the middle of the storm. Rest assured, the Lord is already there in those moments with you. It is also important to know that you can have struggles and still love your babies equally. I don't love her any less, but she does challenge me. My husband would agree, she was given to us to teach us patience and unconditional love.

1. Have you ever felt so hopeless that you didn't think God would show up?

2. What ways did the Lord show you joy during this time?

3. How did you feel when He did show up for you?

THE ULTIMATE TWIN MOM
30-DAY DEVOTIONAL

Dear Heavenly Father-

Lord, You are never far away. You are wonderful and loving. Thank You for always showing up without fail. I never have to question if You are near. This life is full of moments that are hard and challenging and it is those moments that keep us humble. Thank You for all Your blessings. In Jesus's name I give thanks, Amen.

DAY 24

Kindness

*Therefore, as God's chosen ones, holy and dearly
loved, put on compassion, kindness, humility,
gentleness, and patience, bearing with another,
and forgiving one another if anyone has a griev-
ance against another. Just as the Lord has forgiven
you, so you are also to forgive.*
(Colossians 3:12-13, CSB)

My baby shower was the most beautiful one that I
have ever seen. My theme was sloths, which was also
the same as my nursery. There is a sweet peace about
sloths. They are who I want to be. Happy, laid back, and
adorable are just a few attributes. I love the life they live.

I have never seen so many gifts in my life. Our community supported us so beautifully. We literally had
enough diapers to hit a year old. We were loved on so
well. After all these girls were prayed for, for a long time.
Our church family knew about our struggle to get pregnant. We shared our testimony at a freedom retreat. We
had a prayer army behind us.

The shower was so well thought out and planned. It is very evident they put their hearts into it. My cakes were precious, the food was delicious, and the games were fun too! I could not have pictured anything better. Such kindness was shown to us during our entire pregnancy and the following months thereafter. Just know that the Lord has every detail in mind before you even think about it. He is not going to bless you halfway. He is going to work it all out and do it exceedingly.

Our girls were a miracle via IVF. The process was nearly flawless and so smooth. We did a gender reveal video and posted it on Christmas. We had such a fun time filming. The shower was amazing. My cesarean section and healing process was impeccable. I healed quickly. I have virtually no scar. We were able to obtain the formula. God made sure to cover each and every single detail. It was absolutely His loving kindness. And He will show you the same.

1. When was it that you have most felt the Lord's kindness? How about the kindness of others?

2. What ways did the Lord show you joy during this time?

3. Have you been in a position to be used by the Lord as the one exercising kindness.

Dear Heavenly Father-

You are in every single detail of our life. I don't for a moment think that I am doing this on my own. Help us to have the eyes to always see Your kindness as well as others. We love You and are thankful for each and every act of kindness we come across. Lord, help us to never take You for granted. In Jesus's name I give thanks, Amen.

DAY 25

Doubt

*...and every proud thing that is raised up
against the knowledge of God,*
(2 Corinthians 10:5, CSB)

Can we even do this? Be parents? Wake up all hours of the night? For how long? What if they turn out to be not the best adults? Were we even ready for kids? These were just a few of the questions that I began to ask myself almost immediately. Doubt flooded my mind instantly. It was a whirlwind in my mind.

Part of our "birthing plan" was to keep our babies in our room for the entire stay at the hospital. Yes, we were those people. And believe me we did give it our best shot. But it was around 3 a.m. when we realized that we were not getting any sleep with these babies in our room. A sobering feeling that described our unforeseen future. The nurses were so kind. They offered to take them to the nursery for a bit while we slept. So, you better believe we phoned the nurses to come fetch these two crying babies. We had no idea what we were in for. They came and took them for three hours so we could get minimal rest. We also had no idea that those three hours would be the last we would have for a long time.

Right after we got home, we immediately doubted every part of this journey. Everything we did, we were questioning. Did we do it right? Are they eating enough? Are they sleeping enough? Pooping enough? Burping enough? Endless doubt lingered. They don't have classes that teach you how to bring a baby home from the hospital let alone two babies at once.

However, there was one thing that we did not doubt and that was that the Lord was with us. You see doubting our abilities meant we were doubting God's plan for us. Obviously, He deemed us fit and ready to do this. We have to remember that He doesn't call the qualified. He qualifies the called. The ones He personally calls.

So sweet mama, drop all that doubt. Know you are beautifully and wonderfully made, and God has equipped you for this very moment. He picked you. Have confidence, you beautiful soul, that you are the one who can be a better mama to these babies than anyone else on this planet. You got this, and He's got you!

1. What has been your biggest doubt during the beginning months? Has it changed as you and your babies have grown together?

2. What ways did the Lord show you joy during this time?

3. How are you combating that doubt with truth?

Dear Heavenly Father-

Doubting me and my abilities means doubting You and Your plan for me and that is just not something that I am willing to do. Who am I to doubt the creator of the universe? You are love and joy and confidence. You are who I want to be like. Help me to always know You got my back and for that very reason, I rebuke all thoughts of doubt and inadequacy. I love You, Lord.

In Jesus's name I give thanks, Amen.

DAY 26

Marriage

For this reason, a man will leave his father and
mother and the two will become one flesh. So, they
are no longer tow, but one flesh.
(Mark 10:7-8, CSB)

"A baby changes everything." You have probably
heard that before. One of the most cliché yet accurate
statements I have ever heard. It is a powerful one liner
that rings true. And I am not just talking about our bod-
ies. That would be fine if it were just that alone. But it
is everything. Our freedom. Our daily operations. And
most importantly our marriage.

Did you know that your most important human relationship on this planet ever, is your spouse? But I will
be the first to admit that when your babies come alone,
that becomes more of a challenge. It is no walk in the
park, that is for sure. You certainly learn things about
that person that you never knew were a thing. You
would assume that a fourteen-year marriage is fire-

proof. Safe against all things. But then you add children and sleep deprivation to that, and things change fast. Really fast. This is a great reason that premarital counseling is beneficial. It is important to discuss all the important things. And when you think you have discussed everything, discuss it again. Discuss the way in which you want to incorporate discipline. Who might be responsible for what. What you will allow and what you will not allow.

It goes without saying the Lord needs to be the center of it all. That will be your safe place. That will be where you start. Make sure to keep your marriage a priority. Your relationship with your spouse is paramount in raising your children. They will feed off you. They can feel your emotions. It is also important to remember you are on the same team. The minute you lose that footing, you will start to fall apart. So do yourself a favor. Make sure that you are working together to keep your relationship strong as well as your relationship with the Lord intact. Keep your eyes on Him. He will indeed help you and lead you.

1. Has your marriage changed since you have had your babies? In what ways? How did you address those hurdles?

2. What ways did the Lord show you joy during this time?

3. Is there anything that you would change about your marriage since you became a mom? Is there anything that you would have done to better prepare yourself?

Dear Heavenly Father-

You are the one who created marriage. It is in Your will for us to join with our spouses and become one flesh. We are to love and respect each other. Help us to always remember that we are on the same team. So much has changed since these babies came into our lives. Let us to be quick to listen and love and slow to anger. Thank You for my husband. I do love him with all my heart, even in the hard moments. In Jesus's name I give thanks, Amen.

DAY 27

Comparison

*For we don't dare classify or compare ourselves
with some who commend themselves. But in
measure measuring themselves by themselves and
comparing themselves to themselves, they lack
understanding.*
(2 Corinthians, 10:12 CSB)

I know I can't be the only one who scrolls through
social media looking at how the other twin moms get
around. Seeing all these overachievers cooking special
meals for their newly eating babies. Watching all the
toddlers using sign language. Doing all the things I pictured I would be doing as a first-time mom.

As a new parent there are so many things that you
plan to do. You have all these ideas about what parent-
ing should be like. Then you pop on the social media
platforms where there are all these "perfect" blogging
moms that make you feel like you are less than you are.
Those moms who have babies that sleep through the

night at like three months or something. When I am begging for just a few hours. Don't forget the baby-led weaning community. They spend so much time making these photo perfect little balanced meals, working on that "100 foods before 1" goal. And here I am putting chicken nuggets in the air fryer and warming macaroni and cheese in the microwave. For me the first year has been about survival. Don't worry about what everyone else is doing.

Let me tell you that comparison is absolutely the thief of joy. Every single time. You will constantly feel less than if you focus on what everyone else is doing and what you are not doing. You can only do what you can do. Before my girls came, I dreamed of who I would be as a mom. I would exclusively nurse my babies. That did not happen. I only was able to nurse one of them because the other was not interested and only for eight and a half months. I would read books every night and pray over my girls. Well, that didn't happen. Reading was rare and praying was difficult because I was so sleep deprived, I couldn't always remember to do it. I am thankful for God's grace. I would do the baby led weaning, making three meals a day, with a hundred different foods by the time they turned one. My fear of food allergies kept me in a box, limiting me to try new things. I would never lose my temper and always speak with a quiet and peaceful voice. Epic fail there, too. *I bet those Instagram moms never lost their cool,* is what I thought. It is probably just me. Wrong! Nobody usually posts the bad stuff.

The Lord made us perfect and unique in our own ways. Everything will work out and be exactly how it should be. Make sure those babies are healthy, fed, clean and loved. That is all you need to do. Give them babies to the Lord, trust, and know He is in control. You are doing the best you can. And that is enough! And so are you. The Lord loves you right where you are. He knows your struggles. He knows that you are going to make it because His plans for you are perfect ones.

1. Have you ever looked on social media and seen the life that you thought you wanted?

2. What ways did the Lord show you joy during this time?

3. If you could start over, what would you do differently?

Dear Heavenly Father-

Why would I waste another minute comparing my life and blessings to others? Help me to see all the amazingness that is right in front in front of me. Give me confidence to know that I am doing a great job and the best one I can. I love my babies more than anything else. I want what is best for them. And I know You do too. A healthy me means a healthy them. Thank You, Lord, for making me the mom of these beautiful children. In Jesus's name I give thanks, Amen.

DAY 28

Grace

But He said to me, "My grace is sufficient for you
for my power is perfected in weakness." Therefore, I
will most gladly boast all the more about my weak-
nesses so that Christ's power my reside in me.
(2 Corinthians 12:9, CSB)

"Can you grab me that burp rag?" "Never mind, I got it." That is the tune that I have sung for the last year. And when I couldn't do everything all at once, I would get mad at myself. And naturally everyone always had the same exact advice. "Just give yourself grace," but I never really understood it until I did. I have always had a hard time accepting help from others. It is not something that I am proud of, and it doesn't make it easier with how upset I would get if I couldn't. But that is how I have always been. Why is it so hard for me to accept help? I think part of me feels like if someone helps me then I will owe them something in return. And I for sure, hands down, hate "owing" people anything. I have been working on that with the Lord. He has shown me I am worthy to be helped and even that He sends people to help me with no expectation of something in return.

I think that a lot of my independence has to do with my father. He was the man who did it all. He never sat down to take a break. I have a lot of admiration for him in that respect. I think that is why I try to mimic that and do the same. It is always easier for me to do something than it is for me to ask someone to do something that I will have to go behind and redo myself. It is a terrible cycle that is for sure.

I began to pray that the Lord would show me how to show myself grace. I can only do what is in my control. I can't control what anyone else does, only myself. I need to get that in my mind and be loving to myself. The Lord showed me that he continuously shows me grace and so should I. After all this is the creator of the universe that is extending this grace to me. So, if He can, so can I. There is nothing wrong with accepting help. And there is certainly nothing wrong with not doing everything all at once. All that needs to be done will eventually get done. And you need to show yourself grace too. He loves you and He has everything under control. One thing I can promise you is that whatever you can't get to, will still be there when you get around to getting it. You are so loved and so perfect just the way you are.

1. Have you ever been overly hard on yourself? What was the reason you were so upset with yourself?

2. What ways did the Lord show you joy during this time?

3. What have you realized since having two or more babies about your ability to do things? Can you do them like you did before? Are you able to keep up?

Dear Heavenly Father-

You created it all. And You give me grace. I should be able to give myself grace too. I am worth it. We only get one chance to do this life right. Help me to focus on the things I can do and can control and give myself grace for the remaining. I love You and trust You with all my heart. I surrender everything that is out of my control to You, Lord. Thank You for teaching me to have grace. In Jesus's name I give thanks, Amen.

DAY 29

Attitude

Do not be conformed to this age, but be transformed by the renewing of your mind, so that you may discern what is the good, pleasing, and perfect will of God.
(Romans 12:12, CSB)

Let me begin by being completely honest with you, I have always been a little sassy. Probably a little too much for my own good. This is a character trait that has always needed a little work. It is one of those areas that require a little more of a deliberate and intentional change.

After my girls arrived, I became increasingly agitated because I felt like I was constantly failing. It is like standing in the middle of an ocean and getting crushed by a wave knocking you down. As you begin to stand back up, the next wave has already arrived, again knocking you down. So on and so forth. Never being able to actually stand. Never really being able to catch your breath. So, it goes without saying, I have an attitude sometimes.

The reality is I needed to surrender my attitude to the Lord. The last thing I want to do is to raise some sassy little girls with my attitude and I know that. It is important to keep in mind that your children are sponges and they are watching and listening to your every move. As they get older, they will begin to mimic and repeat all the things you say. I certainly don't want to have kids that act like me. The goal needs to be modeling the behavior I want to see.

Fill your home with the love of the Lord. Respond with love, grace, and patience. Patience will make all the difference. It will change the mood of your home. Furthermore, it would definitely make life a lot better. Peace and love are the goal.

1. Have you ever had a bad attitude towards something or someone and you recognized it? What did you do to correct it?

2. What ways did the Lord show you joy during this time?

3. How do you try to fix the negative situations that are created by your attitude?

Dear Heavenly Father-

Lord as a flawed human it is easy to respond with emotion. It is easy to be fast to respond with frustration and irritation. Help me to slow my role. Think before I speak. Breathe before I respond. And remember that I love my babies and my spouse, and they deserve the kindest version of me that I can give them. I love You, Lord. Thank You for always forgiving me. In Jesus's name I give thanks, Amen.

DAY 30

Healing

*My flesh and my heart may fail, but God is the
strength of my heart, my portion forever.*
(Psalms 73:26, CSB)

Throughout our life we will go through many moments of healing whether mental or physical or even both. I always say if you are not in a storm, you are either going in or coming out of one. That is just the way it is. But there is one thing that stands true in that the amazing God we serve will be right by our side. The Bible says when we go through troubles He will be there. In fact, He even says rejoice in your troubles, it is there in that place where we are refined.

Whether you are healing from a natural birth or a cesarean section, you are waiting for physical healing. You are probably ready for the sensitivity to go away, maybe for some bleeding to stop, or even for all that other not so fun stuff that happens when you sacrifice your body for your children. Healing is the goal. My friend, rest your heart and know, healing will come. Continue to be patient and take care of yourself. Drink lots of water. Do the necessary exercises. Be the best you so you can take care of those babies.

Don't forget in the quest to have your body return to some state of normalcy, make sure you watch your mental health. Having two babies at one time is hard for anyone. It will undoubtedly wear on your mental health. If possible, have a support system. Have someone help you if you are able to. Accept the help. Say "yes" to your friends who want to come to your rescue. There is never enough help. I am a year in and when my mother-in-love says she is coming over to help me, you better believe there is a happy dance happening on my end. Take breaks when you can. Breathe. I know how cliché that sounds. It is like that wonderful advice you always get "sleep when they sleep." Sure, it seems ideal but never really feasible. I never had the ability to do that but seriously, rest when you can rest.

Things will get done when they get done. They just don't need to get done all at the same time. Take time to heal. Make sure you make time to speak to your heavenly Father who is never far away. He is the one who understands you most. He is the master physician. Put your worries on Him. He can handle it. He loves you and has the best plans for you and your babies. But take time to heal. Love yourself and love your babies. Give yourself grace. I love you, friend!

1. Did you have a natural birth or a cesarean section? How was your healing process?

2. What ways did the Lord show you joy during this time?

3. What has been the hardest part about healing for you? Physical? Or mental? How have you turned to the Lord during this time?

THE ULTIMATE TWIN MOM
30-DAY DEVOTIONAL

Dear Heavenly Father-

You are the master physician. The one who holds my family's future in your hands. I know I can have confidence that you will heal me from the top of my head to the tips of my toes. Inside and outside of my body. I put my entire physical and mental health into your hands. In Jesus's name I give thanks, Amen.

Notes

THE ULTIMATE TWIN MOM
30-DAY DEVOTIONAL

SHAWNTAE NALLEY

THE ULTIMATE TWIN MOM
30-DAY DEVOTIONAL

SHAWNTAE NALLEY

In Closing

Trust and know that the Lord knew exactly what He was doing when He allowed you to become pregnant with both of those babies. They were made for this perfect moment in your life at this perfect time. Even if you don't always see it, believe it. They are meant to be here, and God has an amazing purpose for your family. He has plans to prosper you. Have faith! Rely on Him. Enjoy those beautiful gifts and that spouse He blessed you with. Know that they were hand-picked by the King of kings for this time.

Time passes so very fast. And we only get one chance at this. Make the moments last. Don't compare yourself to anyone. Don't compare those babies and their progress to any other babies. It will rob you of the joy the Lord has blessed you with. Revel in His blessings as they were intended for you. There is no other mommy on this planet that could be a better mommy to your babies than you can. Keep doing all the amazing things you are doing. He sees you and those babies. Those babies love you beyond words. You are an amazing mom. And your hard work and effort into raising amazing humans is not unnoticed. I love you, friend! If you need someone to vent to or talk to, feel free to email me. I would love to hear from you. I would love to pray for you.

Printed in the USA
CPSIA information can be obtained
at www.ICGtesting.com
LVHW010837111023
760603LV00009B/137